Yummy Oreo Recipes
Cooking Oreo Desserts You Will Love to Eat

DEDICATION

Contents

Oreo Cookie Balls

YIELDS: 24

PREP TIME: 0 HOURS 5 MINS

TOTAL TIME: 2 HOURS 10 MINS

INGREDIENTS

1 (14-oz.) package Oreos

1 (8-oz.) package cream cheese, softened

Pinch kosher salt

1 (12-oz.) package chocolate chips, melted

DIRECTIONS

Use a food processor to crush cookies into fine crumbs.

Add all but 2 tablespoons crushed cookies to a medium bowl. Add cream cheese and and salt and stir until evenly combined.

Line a baking sheet with parchment paper. Using a small cookie scoop, form mixture into small balls and transfer to prepared baking sheet.

Freeze until slightly hardened, about 30 minutes.

Dip frozen balls in melted chocolate until coated and return to baking sheet. Sprinkle with remaining cookie crumbs. Freeze until chocolate hardens, about 15 minutes.

Chocolate-Covered Oreos

YIELDS: 1 DOZEN

PREP TIME: 0 HOURS 10 MINS

TOTAL TIME: 0 HOURS 30 MINS

INGREDIENTS

12 Oreos

1 1/2 c. semisweet chocolate chips, melted

2 tsp. coconut oil, optional

1/4 c. white chocolate chips, melted

DIRECTIONS

Line a small baking sheet with parchment paper. In a medium shallow bowl, stir together melted semisweet chocolate and coconut oil if using. Dip each Oreo in the melted chocolate, then place on the parchment lined baking sheet. Place in the refrigerator to set, 10 minutes.

Use a spoon to drizzle white chocolate onto Oreos. Return to the refrigerator to set, 10 minutes longer.

Giant Oreo Cake

YIELDS: 12

PREP TIME: 0 HOURS 25 MINS

TOTAL TIME: 0 HOURS 45 MINS

INGREDIENTS

FOR THE COOKIE LAYERS

2 1/2 c. all-purpose flour

2 c. granulated sugar

1 c. brown sugar

1 c. dark cocoa powder

2 tsp. baking soda

1/2 tsp. baking powder

1/2 tsp. kosher salt

1 c. butter, softened

2 large eggs

FOR THE FILLING

1/2 c. butter, softened

1/2 c. vegetable shortening

2 tsp. pure vanilla extract

4 c. powdered sugar

DIRECTIONS

Preheat oven to 350°. Line two 8" round cake pans with parchment paper and spray with cooking spray.

In a large bowl, combine flour, sugars, cocoa powder, baking soda, baking powder, and salt and whisk until thoroughly combined. Add butter and mix with a hand mixer on low speed until the dough starts to come together in a mass. Add eggs and mix until thoroughly combined. The mixture should feel sandy.

Press dough into prepared baking pans, then press a large fork around the edges of the cookie to make indentations similar to Oreos. Bake until cookies are slightly crackly on top, about 20 minutes. Let cool in pan for 10 minutes before inverting onto cooling racks to cool completely.

Meanwhile, make filling: In a large bowl, combine butter, vegetable shortening, and vanilla. Beat with a hand mixer until smooth and fluffy. Gradually add sugar, about 1 cup at a time, and mix until smooth.

Gather filling into a large ball then, on a piece of parchment paper, pat it into a large disc approximately 8" in diameter.

Transfer one of the cookie layers to a serving dish. (Save the prettier of the two for the top layer.) Place filling on top of cooled cookie then top with remaining cookie, indentation side-up. Slice into wedges and serve with milk.

Oreogasm Poke Cake

YIELDS: 10

PREP TIME: 0 HOURS 20 MINS

TOTAL TIME: 0 HOURS 45 MINS

INGREDIENTS

1 box chocolate cake mix, plus ingredients called for on box

1 1/2 c. marshmallow crème

1 tbsp. water

1/2 c. finely ground Oreos

2 c. heavy cream

1/2 c. powdered sugar

1/2 tsp. kosher salt

1 c. crushed Oreos, divided

6 Oreos, halved

Chocolate fudge sauce, for garnish

DIRECTIONS

Preheat oven to 350° and grease a 9"-x-13" pan. Prepare chocolate cake mix according to package directions and bake until a toothpick inserted in the center comes out clean, about 25 minutes.

Poke cake all over with the bottom of a wooden spoon. In a small bowl, microwave marshmallow crème and water, then stir until smooth. Stir in ground Oreos, then pour all over cake, making sure to fill the poked holes.

Make frosting: in a large bowl using a hand mixer, beat heavy cream, powdered sugar and salt until medium peaks form. Fold in 1/2 cup crushed Oreos. Frost cake with the whipped cream and sprinkle with the rest of the crushed Oreos. Top with halved Oreos and drizzle with chocolate sauce. Serve.

Oreogasm Cheesecake Bars

YIELDS: 12

PREP TIME: 0 HOURS 20 MINS

TOTAL TIME: 1 HOUR 0 MINS

INGREDIENTS

nonstick cooking spray

1 box fudgy brownie mix, plus ingredients called for on box

15 whole Oreos

3 8-oz. blocks cream cheese, softened

3/4 c. sugar

3 large eggs

1/2 tsp. pure vanilla extract

pinch of kosher salt

15 Oreos, crushed

1/2 c. semisweet chocolate chips, melted

DIRECTIONS

Preheat oven to 350° and line a 9"-x-13" pan with parchment paper. Spray parchment with cooking spray.

Prepare brownie mix according to package directions and pour batter into prepared pan. Place Oreos on brownie batter.

Prepare cheesecake mixture: In a large bowl, beat cream cheese and sugar until fluffy. Add eggs, vanilla, and salt and beat until combined. Fold in crushed Oreos until fully incorporated.

Pour cheesecake mixture over brownie batter and bake until edges are set and center of cheesecake mixture is only slightly jiggly, 37 to 40 minutes.

Let cheesecake brownies cool completely in pan. Drizzle with melted chocolate and white chocolate and serve.

Oreo Party Dunk

YIELDS: 10

PREP TIME: 0 HOURS 10 MINS

TOTAL TIME: 0 HOURS 10 MINS

INGREDIENTS

1 package Oreos

1/3 c. whole milk

1/3 c. white chocolate liquer

1/3 c. Baileys Irish Cream

DIRECTIONS

Open Oreo package and remove all cookies from middle compartment.

Combine milk, white chocolate liqueur and Baileys in the empty compartment

Dip!

Cookie Dough Stuffed Oreos

YIELDS: 30

PREP TIME: 0 HOURS 10 MINS

TOTAL TIME: 1 HOUR 35 MINS

INGREDIENTS

1/2 c. (1 stick) melted butter

1/2 c. granulated sugar

1/2 c. packed brown sugar

1 tsp. pure vanilla extract

1 c. almond flour

1/2 tsp. kosher salt

2/3 c. mini chocolate chips

24 Oreos

1 c. chocolate chips

1 tbsp. coconut oil

1/4 c. sprinkles

DIRECTIONS

Line a large baking sheet with parchment paper. In a large bowl, whisk together melted butter, sugars, and vanilla. Stir in almond flour and salt, then fold in mini chocolate chips.

Separate Oreos trying to keep creme intact. Place 2 tsp of cookie dough on Oreo half with creme, then sandwich with other half of Oreo. Repeat with remaining Oreos and dough.

Place chocolate chips and coconut oil in a microwave safe bowl and microwave in 30 second intervals until melted. Dip Oreos halfway into chocolate, place on prepared baking sheet, and top with sprinkles. Refrigerate until chocolate is hardened, 1 hour.

Minion Oreos

YIELDS: 12

PREP TIME: 0 HOURS 5 MINS

TOTAL TIME: 0 HOURS 25 MINS

INGREDIENTS

2 c. white chocolate chips

1 tbsp. coconut oil

Yellow food coloring

12 Oreos

Black cookie icing

Candy eyeballs

DIRECTIONS

Line a baking sheet with parchment. In a medium bowl, combine white chocolate chips, coconut oil and 4 to 5 drops yellow food coloring. Microwave on 50 percent power in 30 second intervals until the chocolate has melted. Stir until smooth.

Using a fork, toss each Oreo in the yellow chocolate mixture until fully coated and transfer to the baking sheet. Let chocolate set and harden, about 10 minutes.

Use cookie icing to pipe glasses and mouth, then press candy eyes on top of glasses./

Polar Bear Paw Cupcakes

YIELDS: 18

PREP TIME: 0 HOURS 20 MINS

TOTAL TIME: 0 HOURS 40 MINS

INGREDIENTS

1 box chocolate cake mix, plus ingredients called for on box

1 can vanilla frosting

3 c. sweetened shredded coconut

9 oreos

72 Brown m&ms

DIRECTIONS

Preheat oven to 350° and line two cupcake pans with 18 cupcake liners. Prepare cake mix according to package instructions.

Bake until a toothpick inserted into the center of the cupcakes comes out clean, 20 to 25 minutes. Let cupcakes cool completely.

Add coconut to a shallow bowl. Using a small offset spatula (or a knife) spread frosting onto the cupcakes then dip the tops in the coconut.

Twist Oreos apart so that you have 18 halves. Place an Oreo half on top of each cupcake, then place 4 brown M&Ms on top of the Oreos to make the paws.

Mint Oreo Bark

YIELDS: 8 - 10

PREP TIME: 0 HOURS 10 MINS

TOTAL TIME: 3 HOURS 10 MINS

INGREDIENTS

25 oz. white chocolate chips

1 tsp. coconut oil

green food coloring

20 Oreos, crushed and divided

1 tsp. peppermint extract

1/2 c. semisweet chocolate chips, melted

DIRECTIONS

Line a large baking sheet with parchment paper. In a large bowl, combine white chocolate, coconut oil and green food coloring. Microwave on high for 25 seconds at a time, stirring after each time until chocolate chips are completely melted.

Add 3/4 of crushed Oreos and peppermint extract to melted chocolate. Fold to combine. Pour onto prepared baking sheet and spread in an even layer. Top with remaining crushed Oreos and drizzle with melted chocolate.

Place in the refrigerator to harden for 2 to 3 hours. Break into pieces and serve.

Peppermint Oreo Truffles

YIELDS: 20

PREP TIME: 0 HOURS 15 MINS

TOTAL TIME: 0 HOURS 45 MINS

INGREDIENTS

1 (15.5-oz.) package Oreos, crushed

1 (8-oz. package) cream cheese, softened to room temperature

12 candy canes, crushed, divided

2 c. chocolate chips, melted

2 tsp. coconut oil

DIRECTIONS

Line a small baking sheet with parchment paper. In a large bowl, combine crushed Oreos with cream cheese and half the crushed candy canes. Stir until cream cheese is completely integrated into the Oreo crumbs.

Using a small cookie scoop, form Oreo mixture into small balls and place on the cooking sheet. Repeat until all Oreo mixture is used and place baking sheet in freezer for 10 minutes.

Meanwhile, mix coconut oil with melted chocolate chips. When the balls are chilled, dip them in the chocolate and place back on cooking sheet. Sprinkle with remaining crushed candy canes and return to the freezer to harden, 10 more minutes.

No-Bake Oreo Cheesecake

YIELDS: 8

PREP TIME: 0 HOURS 10 MINS

TOTAL TIME: 4 HOURS 10 MINS

INGREDIENTS

1 1/2 c. Heavy cream, whipped

12 oz. cream cheese, softened

1/2 c. sugar

1 package crushed Oreos, plus more to top

DIRECTIONS

In a large bowl, combine whipped heavy cream with softened cream cheese and sugar and stir until completely combined. (If cream cheese clumps remain, transfer mixture to a stand mixer or use a hand mixer.

Fold in crushed Oreos.

Pour mixture into prepared pie crust, smoothing over top with a rubber spatula. Top with more crushed Oreos, cover with plastic wrap, and refrigerate until firm, at least 4 hours.

Cookie Monster Oreos

YIELDS: 12

PREP TIME: 0 HOURS 10 MINS

TOTAL TIME: 0 HOURS 20 MINS

INGREDIENTS

2 c. white chocolate chips

1 tbsp. coconut oil

Blue food coloring

12 oreos

Blue sanding sugar

24 Candy eyes

Mini chocolate chip cookies, for garnish

DIRECTIONS

Line a baking sheet with parchment or wax paper.

In a medium bowl, combine white chocolate chips, coconut oil and 4 to 5 drops of blue food coloring. Microwave on 50% power in 30 second intervals until the chocolate has melted. Stir until smooth.

Toss each Oreo cookie in the blue chocolate mixture until fully coated and transfer to the baking sheet. Sprinkle immediately with sanding sugar then stick two candy eyes on top. Let the chocolate set completely before serving, about 10 minutes.

Oreo Penguins

YIELDS: 12

PREP TIME: 0 HOURS 10 MINS

TOTAL TIME: 0 HOURS 20 MINS

INGREDIENTS

12 oreos

2 c. chocolate chips, melted

2 tbsp. coconut oil

24 Candy eyes

6 orange M&Ms, halved

12 white candy melts

12 round peppermint candies, halved

2 Twizzler candies, cut into 2" pieces

DIRECTIONS

Line a baking sheet with parchment paper. In a medium bowl, whisk together melted chocolate and coconut oil. Using a spoon, dunk Oreos in chocolate and toss until fully coated in chocolate. Transfer to the baking sheet.

To each Oreo, place 2 candy eyes on top and place a white candy melt below. Place peppermint candy halves on both sides of the eyes then place the Twizzler piece on top. Let set in the refrigerator for 10 minutes.

Oreogasm Dip

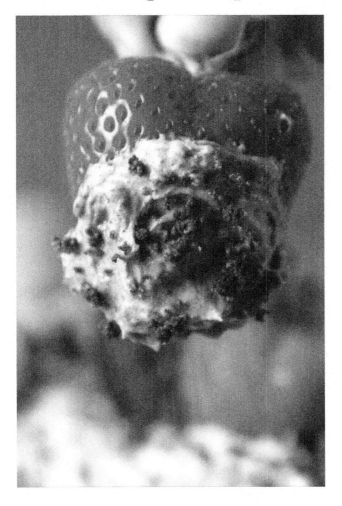

YIELDS: 10

PREP TIME: 0 HOURS 15 MINS

TOTAL TIME: 0 HOURS 15 MINS

INGREDIENTS

8 oz. cream cheese, softened

1 c. powdered sugar

3 c. whipped topping (like Cool Whip)

3 c. crushed Oreos, divided

Whole Oreos, for garnish

Strawberries, for serving

Green apple slices, for serving

Graham crackers, for serving

DIRECTIONS

In a large bowl using a hand mixer, mix cream cheese and powdered sugar until smooth. Fold in whipped topping and 2 1/2 cups crushed Oreos until smooth.

Transfer to a serving bowl and top with remaining crushed Oreos. Garnish with a whole Oreo and a halved strawberry, and serve with more strawberries, apple slices, and graham crackers.

Easiest Oreo Ice Cream Tart

YIELDS: 6

PREP TIME: 0 HOURS 10 MINS

TOTAL TIME: 0 HOURS 40 MINS

INGREDIENTS

30 Oreo cookies, frosting scraped

1 stick melted butter

12 scoops cookies 'n cream ice cream

2 Hershey's Cookies 'n Creme bars, melted

Chocolate sauce, for drizzling

DIRECTIONS

In a food processor fitted with a metal blade, pulse cookies until they resemble fine crumbs, then add melted butter and process until combined.

Transfer Oreo crust to a 9" springform pan and press in crust until firmly packed. Freeze until firm, at least 30 minutes.

When ready to serve, remove springform pan and scoop ice cream over tart. Drizzle with cookies 'n creme bars and chocolate syrup. Slice and serve. (If the ice cream seems too soft to slice, freeze 10 minutes to let it firm up.)

Funfetti Fried Oreos

YIELDS: 16

PREP TIME: 0 HOURS 10 MINS

COOK TIME: 0 HOURS 30 MINS

TOTAL TIME: 0 HOURS 40 MINS

INGREDIENTS

BIRTHDAY CAKE FRIED OREOS

1 bottle vegetable oil (16 oz or larger)

1 c. pancake mix (like Bisquick)

1 c. white or Funfetti cake mix

1 c. milk

1 tsp. vanilla extract

2 eggs

1 package Oreos

SUGAR-SPRINKLE GLAZE

1 c. powdered sugar

1/4 c. buttermilk (or regular milk)

1/3 c. rainbow sprinkles

DIRECTIONS

Make the Birthday Cake Fried Oreos: Fill a deep-walled skillet about 1 1/2 inches high with vegetable oil. Place over medium-high heat. As it heats, pour pancake mix, cake mix, milk, vanilla extract and eggs into a large mixing bowl. Whisk to combine, breaking up any large lumps.

If you stick the handle of a wooden spoon into the oil, the oil should bubble up and sizzle around it. That's how you know it's ready to fry (that, or a thermometer reads 350 degrees F).

Use tongs to dip the Oreos in the birthday cake mixture, then place each one into the hot oil.

After about 30-45 seconds, flip the Oreos to let the other sides to turn lightly golden.

Place the fried Oreos on a plate lined with paper towels to drain any excess grease.

Make the Sugar-Sprinkle Glaze: Pour the powdered sugar and buttermilk into a soup bowl. Whisk to combine, adding more buttermilk—if necessary—to make it easily pourable. (It should be about the thickness of glue.)

Drizzle glaze over fried Oreos, topping them with sprinkles. Serve.

Oreo Lush

YIELDS: 8 - 10

PREP TIME: 0 HOURS 20 MINS

TOTAL TIME: 6 HOURS 20 MINS

INGREDIENTS

3 c. heavy cream

1 c. powdered sugar

24 Oreos, crushed (about 1/2 package)

48 whole Oreos (about 1 package)

2 boxes instant chocolate pudding, prepared according to package directions

1/2 c. chocolate sauce

DIRECTIONS

Make Oreo whipped cream: In a large bowl using a hand mixer or the bowl of a stand mixer using the whisk attachment, beat cream until medium peaks form. Add powdered sugar and beat until smooth, then fold in 2 cups crushed Oreos.

In a 9"-x-13" baking dish, spread a thin layer of Oreo whipped cream (to help the Oreos stay in place!). Top with a layer of whole Oreos, then add a layer of chocolate pudding, a thick layer of Oreo whipped cream, and a generous drizzle of chocolate sauce. Repeat, ending with the Oreo whipped cream. Top with remaining 1/2 cup crushed Oreos and cover loosely with plastic wrap.

Refrigerate at least 6 hours and up to overnight to let the Oreos soften.

When ready to serve, drizzle with more chocolate sauce.

Oreo Chip Cookies

YIELDS: 15 SERVINGS

PREP TIME: 0 HOURS 15 MINS

COOK TIME: 0 HOURS 15 MINS

TOTAL TIME: 0 HOURS 30 MINS

INGREDIENTS

2 sticks butter, softened

1 c. granulated sugar

1 c. firmly packed light brown sugar

2 large eggs

2 tsp. vanilla extract

1 tsp. baking soda

2 1/2 c. all-purpose flour

1 tsp. salt

1 1/2 c. crushed chocolate wafer cookies (such as Oreos)

DIRECTIONS

Preheat oven to 350 degrees F. Line two large baking sheets with parchment paper.

In a large bowl, combine butter and sugars. Beat with a handmixer until light and fluffy. Add eggs one at a time, and beat until evenly combined. Stir in vanilla.

In a small bowl, whisk together baking soda, flour and salt. Add the dry ingredients to the wet ingredients and stir until just combined.

Using a medium-sized ice cream scoop, place mounds of cookie dough on a the baking sheets, about 2 inches apart. (The cookies will spread.) Bake for about 10-12, until the edges of the cookies begin to turn golden.

Let cool for 5 minutes on baking sheet, then transfer cookies to a wire rack to cool completely.

Peppermint Oreo Milkshake

YIELDS: 1

PREP TIME: 0 HOURS 10 MINS

TOTAL TIME: 0 HOURS 10 MINS

INGREDIENTS

1 candy cane, crushed

3 scoops mint chip ice cream

4 Peppermint Thin Oreos, divided

1/2 c. whole milk

whipped cream, for garnish

DIRECTIONS

Dip rim of glass in water, then crushed candy canes.

In a blender, blend ice cream, 3 Oreos, and milk until smooth. (Add more milk for a thinner consistency.)

Pour milkshake into glass and garnish with whipped cream and crushed Oreo.

Oreo Brownie Pie

YIELDS: 8

PREP TIME: 0 HOURS 20 MINS

TOTAL TIME: 4 HOURS 25 MINS

INGREDIENTS

FOR THE CRUST

1 tube pre-made chocolate chip cookie dough

FOR THE PUDDING

2/3 packet instant chocolate pudding mix

1 1/2 c. whole milk

1 package Oreo cookies

FOR THE WHIPPED CREAM

1 container Cool Whip (8 oz.)

1/3 packet instant chocolate pudding mix

1/2 c. crumbled brownie pieces (either store-bought or leftover homemade ones)

chocolate sauce

DIRECTIONS

Make the crust: Preheat oven to 350° and grease the bottom and sides of a 9" pie plate. Cover with chocolate chip cookie dough and bake for 16 to18 minutes. Shortly after taking it out of the oven, use a measuring cup to press down dough so it forms a gooey crust. Place in the refrigerator to cool.

Make the pudding: Whisk 2/3 packet of pudding mix with milk. Refrigerate 5 minutes to set, then pour into cooled cookie crust. Cover pudding with a layer of Oreo cookies.

Make the whipped cream: In another bowl, mix Cool Whip with remaining 1/3 packet pudding mix. Fold in crumbled brownies, and pour the mixture on top of the pie. Garnish with more brownie pieces. Refrigerate for 4 hours, then drizzle with chocolate sauce just before serving.

Golden Oreo Truffles

YIELDS: 40

PREP TIME: 0 HOURS 45 MINS

TOTAL TIME: 2 HOURS 0 MINS

INGREDIENTS

1 14-oz. package Golden Oreos

8 oz. brick-style cream cheese (full fat)

12 oz. white chocolate, coarsely chopped

Gold sprinkles

DIRECTIONS

Place cookies (whole cookie—including cream center) in a food processor and pulse until crushed into fine crumbs. Pour crumbs into a medium bowl. Add cream cheese, then beat with a handheld or stand mixer fitted with a paddle attachment on medium speed until completely blended.

Roll cookie mixture into 40 balls, about 1" in diameter. Place each onto a lined baking sheet. If mixture is too soft to neatly roll, refrigerate for 30 minutes.

Once rolled, refrigerate balls for at least 1 hour. You need extra firm balls before coating.

Begin melting white chocolate when balls are just about finished chilling. You can melt chocolate in a double boiler or microwave. If using microwave, place chocolate in medium heat-proof bowl. Melt in 30 second increments in microwave, stirring after each increment until completely melted and smooth. Let warm chocolate sit for 5 minutes to slightly cool before dipping.

Remove balls from refrigerator and dip them in white chocolate. Place balls back onto baking sheet after you dip each one. Top dipped truffles with sprinkles. Allow chocolate to completely set in the refrigerator.

Oreo Magic Bars

YIELDS: 15

COOK TIME: 0 HOURS 25 MINS

TOTAL TIME: 0 HOURS 30 MINS

INGREDIENTS

30 Oreo cookies

6 tbsp. butter, melted

can sweetened condensed milk

3/4 c. semisweet chocolate chips

3/4 c. peanut butter chips

1 1/3 c. sweetened coconut flakes

1 c. mini Oreos

DIRECTIONS

Preheat oven to 350 degrees F. Grease a 8x11" pan with cookie spray.

Make Oreo crust: In a food processor fitted with a metal blade, pulse cookies until they resemble fine crumbs, then add melted butter and process until combined. (Alternatively, you can crush the cookies in a large resealable plastic bag using a rolling pin. Transfer cookies to a bowl, and stir in melted butter). The texture should be similar to wet sand.

Press the Oreo-butter mixture into the pan until firmly packed. Pour the sweetened condensed milk on top to cover the crust. Sprinkle with coconut, chocolate chips and peanut butter chips. Then distribute mini Oreos on top. Bake for 20-25 minutes, until the edges of the bars begin to turn golden.

Let cool to room temperature before slicing.

Oreo Coal

YIELDS: 38 - 40

TOTAL TIME: 1 HOUR 15 MINS

INGREDIENTS

40 oreos

1 (8-oz.) block cream cheese, softened

16 oz. semisweet or melting chocolate

1/3 c. Oreo cookies, crushed (or cocoa powder)

DIRECTIONS

Using a food processor fitted with the blade attachment, grind Oreos into crumbs. Transfer crumbs to a medium bowl and add cream cheese. Use a fork to mix until well combined.

Using about one tablespoon of the mixture per ball, form misshapen balls of the Oreo mixture. Place them on a plate and into the fridge for about 30 minutes to 1 hour to firm up.

Microwave melting chocolate in 10 to 15 second increments until melted and smooth. Using a fork or toothpick, dip each Oreo ball into the melted chocolate, then set onto parchment paper. Sprinkle immediately with crushed Oreos, if using, or let dry completely.

If using cocoa powder, once firm, dip your fingers into the cocoa and lightly rub onto Oreo balls to complete the "coal" look. Store balls in the fridge until ready to serve.

Oreo Spider Webs

YIELDS: 18

PREP TIME: 0 HOURS 20 MINS

TOTAL TIME: 0 HOURS 20 MINS

INGREDIENTS

1/4 lb. semi-sweet chocolate, chopped

1/4 lb. white chocolate, chopped

18 Double Stuf Oreo cookies

DIRECTIONS

Line baking sheet with parchment paper and set aside.

Line work surface with wax paper or foil and place wire rack on top. Portion 4 tablespoons of each chocolate and place in plastic bag; snip off one corner and set aside.

In a microwave-safe bowl, melt all but 4 tablespoons each chocolate in 15 second bursts, stirring between each heating.

Working in batches of 2 to 3 Oreos, dip each in chocolate until fully coated and transfer to wire rack. (Lightly scrape the bottom of each cookie against edge of bowl to remove excess coating.)

Melt remaining chocolate and place each color in a plastic bag. Snip a bottom corner and pipe three circles on the opposite-colored cookie.

Using a toothpick and starting from the inner-most circle, drag a line through each circle toward the edge of cookie to create web. Repeat until all cookies are dipped and decorated, then transfer to the refrigerator to set.

Printed in Great Britain
by Amazon

40977776R00036